To Rebecca, Thanks for your endorsement, Judy Suiter

THE RIPPLE EFFECT
HOW THE GLOBAL MODEL OF ENDORSEMENT
OPENS THE DOORS TO SUCCESS

by JUDY SUITER
with Chris Carey

Competitive Edge, Inc.
P.O. Box 2418 • Peachtree City, GA
www.competitiveedgeinc.com

ISBN 0-9721790-2-X

Library of Congress Control Number: TX 6-
023-370

TABLE OF CONTENTS

DEDICATION

To the newest blessing in my life, my grandson, Blake Palmer Suiter.

ACKNOWLEDGMENTS

My life's work and passion has been built upon the endorsements given to me by many people over the past two decades. Without these people who were willing to put their time, energy, professional expertise and reputations "on the line" for me, I would not have been able to pursue my life's mission.

First, I would like to acknowledge Eileen Tooley, who, since my first day in business, has guided me on the technological and financial components that have kept me in business. Being able to find someone with the personal ethics that you can trust unconditionally is rare in today's world; Eileen is that person and it has been a true privilege to have her by my side for the past twenty years.

In 1981, Emory Lewis, CEO of Fayette State Bank, was willing to grant me a $5,000 loan to start my company even though he knew I had no experience in running a company or in the human resources field. Many years later, Emory told me that he never once doubted my ability to be successful. Later, Ron Duffey, CEO and President of Peachtree National Bank supported me with similar financial assistance and became one of my clients and strongest supporters as well. Thank you, Emory and Ron.

After launching my new business in 1982, I asked Peggy Baker, a dear friend who also is a master networker, to introduce me to some of her contacts. Peggy introduced me to Marie Dodd, Vice President of Ivan Allen Company in Atlanta, Georgia and from that meeting; a number of relationships were formed that continue to enrich my business and my life today. Kim Walton, one of those people, is now Senior Vice President of The Bankers Bank and she continues to give me referrals and her friendship. Debbie Sessions of Porter, Keadle Moore; Larry Evans and Debi Truelove of Crisp Hughes Evans; Len Green and Karlene Bauer of Green Holman Frenia & Company; Randy Averett and Ann Cotton of Warren, Averett, Kimbrough & Marino; Jack Salvetti and Nancy Schell of S.R. Snodgrass; Linda Pappajohn of SantoraBuffone CPA Group and Kim Fantaci at the Association for Accounting Administration are just some of the clients that grew out of that initial meeting with Marie Dodd that was set up by Peggy Baker.

I am particularly indebted to my clients, many of whom have been with me since my earliest days and whom I would like to recognize for their loyalty and support. John Taylor has contracted my services through four different companies and continues to be one of my strongest advocates; Ike Reighard, Nancy Blythe, Trace Brigante, Nick Mantia, Terry Nelson and Ruby Swann of HomeBanc Mortgage Corporation; Bill Brockwell, Bruce Clements and Mary Sue Harper from the Federal Law Enforcement Training Center; Marlene Stauffer at Ralston Foods, and Jim Cecil of James P. Cecil and Company, Inc., who have generously supported my endeavors for many years.

A new and exciting dimension of my business in 2002 was our expansion into international markets. For this I would like to thank Gavin Dereaux, Peter Gomez, Henk Kalkman, Edouard Levit, Attila Juhasz, Nik Plevan, Neil Powell, Roy Ramdjanamsingh, Audrey Trachtman, Gabriella Varga, and John Wigham for the parts they played in this successful effort.

In addition to the aforementioned individuals and corporations, there are a few people that also deserve to be recognized for the support and faith they have shown me. Dr. Betty Siegel, President of Kennesaw State University, has provided mentoring and friendship for over twenty years. Additional people whom I would like to acknowledge for their contributions to my work and my life are as follows: Bill Allen, Lisa Baird, Laurie Bogdas, Larry Breed, Hope Cheeks, David Goodwill, Fred Huyghue, Cheryl Marr, Terry McMillian, Rich and Joy Ruhmann, Toni Signoretti, Mark Welker, and Ira Wolfe.

Last, but definitely not least, my staff—Darbie Bufford, Lynn "Iggy" Kahl and Carol Schug; my editor and friend Janet Boyce; my oldest son—Brett and his wife Keely and my youngest son—Drew and his wife Karen, all deserve a very special thanks for putting up with me for all those crazy profiles. And to you, my sister Linda—I owe you one and I love you.

INTRODUCTION

This book is an explanation and study of "en-dorsement"—how it is gained and lost, given and received, utilized and neglected.

What does it mean to endorse? Here are the four definitions provided to us by *The American Heritage Dictionary*:

endorse *(en·dôrs)***:**
1. To write one's signature on the back of (a check, for example) as evidence of the legal **transfer of its ownership**, especially in return for the cash or credit indicated on its face.
2. To place (one's signature), as on a contract, to **indicate approval** of its contents or terms.
3. To **acknowledge** (receipt of payment) by signing a bill, draft, or other instrument.
4. To **give approval** of or **support** to, especially **by public statement**; sanction: endorse a political candidate.

• When you deposit or cash a check at your bank, the cashier looks at the front to see the signature of the originator. It's a statement that funds are available to make the paper check as acceptable as cash in the transaction. The signature *authorizes the transfer of ownership* .

• Then the cashier turns the check over to inspect your signature or endorsement stamp on the back. Your identifying mark doesn't just indicate that the money should be credited to your account. It *signifies* that you are entitled to deposit this check into this account, *states* that the funds are available to back that check, and *guarantees* that, as the depositor, you will make good on any problem the bank might have in collecting those funds.

"Endorsement" can be a legal term—that's what they call it when you sign a contract. It means you *approve the terms* and *pledge yourself* to fulfill all obligations in the agreement.

When you finish a meal and your server presents the bill, your endorsing signature on the credit card slip *acknowledges that you have received value* and *releases resources* to pay for it.

For purposes of this book, we'll examine endorsement as the *approval* and *support* of one who is in a position of influence that advances the purposes and goals of others. We'll look at what endorsement *transfers, guarantees, approves* and *pledges.* And we'll look at how it impacts the outcome of projects, products, companies, institutions, and even nations in terms of *value* and *resources.*

Obviously, endorsement works to the benefit of people who possess it and to the detriment of those who lack it. You can be a *manager* and not have endorsement, but you cannot be a *leader* without it.

The presence or absence of endorsement accounts for success or failure in many situations. It is a requirement for individuals who want to progress in their careers and relationships.

People who gain endorsement achieve greater acceptance for their goals and ideas. They enjoy expanded influence. When individuals have endorsement, they will *automatically* be provided with necessary resources.

Our purpose in writing *The Ripple Effect* is to provide more than examples of endorsement in action. That's the easy part. Our goal is to reveal a practical, working model that explains the mechanics of endorsement—*how* and *why* it works.

When we've finished, you will understand why "some have it and some don't." Even better, the model will teach and demonstrate how you can be one who does!

"Outstanding leaders go out of their way to boost the self-esteem of their personnel. If people believe in themselves, it's amazing what they can accomplish."
— *Sam Walton, Founder of Wal-Mart*

"A leader takes people where they want to go. A great leader takes people where they don't necessarily want to go but ought to be."
— *Rosalynn Carter, America's First Lady*

"Example is not the main thing in influencing others. It's the only thing."
— *Albert Schweitzer, Medical Missionary*

CHAPTER 1: SOURCES & RESOURCES OF ENDORSEMENT

Endorsement is the approval, backing, or support of a person, organization, or thing by means of *pledging one's own assets.*

The assets we pledge in *giving* (or gain in *receiving)* endorsement may include the following:

- money
- time
- talents
- contacts
- reputation
- energy

Endorsement is *reciprocal,* not simply transactional, which means it's a lot more than swapping contacts or business leads. It's about investing your personal reputation and credibility in someone else's cause. It isn't self-oriented or self-promoting, anymore than trust is self-promoting.

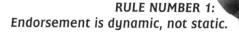

RULE NUMBER 1:
Endorsement is dynamic, not static.

A "balance sheet" relationship exists that includes making ongoing "deposits" as well as "withdrawals." I said it's *reciprocal* because it can exist only in an atmosphere of *trust,* and breaching trust explains why you've seen some people move so quickly from *hero* to *zero.*

Rule #1 states that endorsement is dynamic, not static. This means its value is subject to change. It can be invested profitably, spent, lost, squandered, appreciated, depreciated, devalued, and even bankrupted. Endorsement is a way of expressing the worth of someone's "personal stock." When the right person endorses you, your stock goes up. When you lose endorsement, your stock plummets—at least in that particular market.

Without understanding the nature and power of endorsement, people may invest it carelessly or undervalue it when it is invested on their behalf. It should be prized as a precious resource.

At the same time, endorsement isn't something you can hoard. It is most valuable and does the most good when it's circulated. Receiving credible endorsement within someone else's circle of influence opens previously closed doors for you. And within your own circle of influence, you are able to open doors for others as you lend them your energy, reputation, time, contacts, talents, or money.

Perhaps someone you know is a

member of a business networking group. In such organizations, there are usually weekly meetings in which members swap business cards and explain their products and services to each other. The idea is that, as members promote their own businesses, they will meet people who are potential customers for others in the networking group. So, they carry each other's contact information and refer prospects to each other.

While there is demonstrated value in belonging to some of these groups, giving a casual referral or passing on contact information isn't the same as providing (or receiving) endorsement. It's as different as saying, "I'm in a group with a real estate agent you can talk to about finding a house," or saying, "I've used this agent, and I personally recommend her along with the quality of service she'll provide!" Which person would you rather have working for you? You're further ahead in a networking group when you build relationships of trust that enable you to gain and give true endorsement.

It's important that you see and understand how endorsement works in small, everyday events as well as in weighty, significant opportunities. The ability to gain and grant endorsement can make or break careers and relationships.

For example, in business, the great majority of career opportunities are not advertised in the newspaper. They are filled through referrals, either from inside the hiring company or from headhunting firms that screen and then endorse qualified applicants for the final hiring decision. In relationships, many of us know married couples who met on a blind date set up by someone they trusted. Their relationship might not have been possible except that one person's influence and endorsement opened a door.

Working through the dynamics of endorsement is worthwhile. Endorsement has its rewards:

• When INDIVIDUALS have endorsement, they will always be provided the resources necessary to maintain or improve their own *lifestyle*.

For instance, if an individual who has high endorsement loses a job, five or six people begin looking for employment opportunities and making introductions on this person's behalf.

Certain athletes receive better treatment from game officials than others do. Some baseball players are granted the benefit of the doubt when umpires call balls and strikes. Some basketball players receive more latitude when personal fouls are called. Some soccer players' offenses are allowed while other players are carded for the same behavior. You get the idea—strictness or leniency is sometimes better understood as an indication of personal or professional endorsement.

When people with high endorsement start a new business, it's easier for them to find financial backing, recruit worthy business associates, and attract preferred customers. Individuals who lack endorsement are asked to provide additional data, validation, price concessions, or references to support their position.

• When ORGANIZATIONS have endorsement, they will always be provided the resources necessary to maintain or improve their *growth.*

If companies have endorsement, they enjoy an ample supply of knowledgeable, high-quality applicants who want to work for them and help them grow. Bragging rights come with being employed by prestigious companies, so when Enron and Arthur Anderson enjoyed an excellent reputation, their names were used by employees and service providers to gain favor. When those companies fell from grace, people quickly disassociated themselves.

A company's value, its accessibility to loans and financial resources, and the confidence of its customers, stockholders, and employees is influenced by endorsement. Some businesses gain endorsement through external award programs, such as the J.D. Power Awards based on customer satisfaction surveys. Employee of the Month programs provide internal recognition for top performers. Product manufacturers often pursue Underwriters Laboratory certification or the Good Housekeeping seal as validation of their products' quality.

Here in Georgia, annual "Best of Atlanta" awards celebrate excellence in everything from restaurants to birthday party magicians. The front window of a suburban Chinese restaurant displays a sign referring to its past glory: "Best of Atlanta Award Winner, 1996." Current endorsement is powerful, but outdated endorsement doesn't pack much of a punch.

Endorsement means more when it is credible, and sometimes understatement beats hyperbole. Years ago, several Brooklyn pizzerias competed for customers in side-by-side locations. One restaurant put up a sign that claimed "Best Pizza in New York!" Not to be outdone, the next shop put up a sign that read, "Best Pizza in the World!" A third competitor's announced "Best Pizza in the Universe!" But the fourth pizzeria's sign beat them all by making a more reasonable and easily verified claim: "Best Pizza on the Block!"

• When NATIONS have endorsement, they will always be provided the resources necessary to maintain or improve their *standard of living.*

The Cuban Missile Crisis in the early 1960s cost Cuba its endorsement from the United States. The result of Fidel Castro's permitting installation of Soviet missiles within striking distance of the U.S. was a travel and trade embargo, instituted by President Kennedy, that extends to today, costing Cuba's economy hundreds of billions of U.S. dollars. For years, Castro banked on direct support from the Soviet

Union, but its collapse removed his most influential endorser. As relaxed tensions create openings for increased U.S. aid and tourism to Cuba, watch how "nations with endorsement are provided with resources to maintain or improve their lifestyle."

The United Nations' failure to prosecute Iraq for the deaths of 200,000 Kurds in the 1990s lost it international endorsement. In 2003, the U.N. Security Council's inability to reach consensus regarding Iraqi disarmament and inspection agreements raised questions about its viability as a peacekeeper. These events resulted in calls for a decrease in funding by the U.S., its largest underwriter, as some policy makers asked, "What are we paying for, anyhow?"

France's support of Iraq in the U.N. resulted in widespread anti-French sentiment in the U.S., as Americans dumped French wines down their drains, switched from Michellin tires to other brands, quenched their thirst with anything but Perrier, and swapped french fries in favor of "freedom fries" and "patriot potatoes." France felt its loss of endorsement economically. A nation's loss of endorsement affects the lifestyle of its citizens and businesses too. Whether you agree politically, you can see that there are times when giving endorsement to others costs the endorser its own endorsement with others.

In contrast, consider how Israel benefits from U.S. endorsement in financial aid, military protection, and favored nation status. Israel is permitted to develop advanced nuclear power applications. The lifestyle of Israelis is far better than other inhabitants of the region. Again, we're not examining moral justifications for any of such political decisions. Rather, these examples demonstrate how endorsement affects living standards for nations and their citizens.

Finally, let's look at Iceland, a country that enjoys prosperity because it has become a leader in information technology management. Iceland committed itself to creating a 100 percent literate citizenry so its workforce would be regarded as exceptionally capable, educated, intelligent, and efficient. It developed a strategy to wire the entire country for high-speed data access so it could compete for business as a world-class information processor and distributor. As a result, Iceland has won more than its share of international technology and data support contracts. It enjoys a reputation for both language and computer literacy. At one time, Iceland's geographic isolation would have prevented it from developing foreign markets. Today, the Internet has leveled the playing field, enabling this country inside the Arctic Circle to work anywhere in the world with companies that outsource and maintain their business records off-property.

Again, endorsement always provides necessary resources, whether for individuals, organizations, or nations. And lack of endorsement equals a lack of resources.

CHAPTER 2: ELEMENTS THAT IMPACT ENDORSEMENT

In the mid-70s, Zig Ziglar's book, *See You At The Top,* cited a university study revealing that 15% of an individual's ability to *get* a job, *keep* a job, and *move ahead* in the job could be attributed directly to technical skills. Surprisingly, the remaining 85% of job success depended on skill with people.

Occasionally, someone questions whether this statistic is still relevant in today's technically advanced culture. The answer is yes—in my consulting work, I've found that applying *high-touch* solutions to *high-tech* problems is often the difference between success or failure for a client or a project.

As you read this chapter and gain a better understanding of The Endorsement Model, consider how the scales tip toward people, companies, and countries that understand and apply these "people skill" concepts for increased endorsement resulting in improved performance.

RULE NUMBER 2: Performance is directly proportional to endorsement.

Five factors impact a person's, an organization's, and a country's ability to gain endorsement. As you identify them, you'll know why some people have endorsement and others don't. You'll also see that they are not items on a buffet from which you pick and choose—you'll want all of them!

1. COMPETENCE

• **TECHNICAL:** Beyond just demonstrating expertise in specific fields, added personal qualities of reliability and resourcefulness create a climate that encourages endorsement. Do you know how a technology works and can you make it do what it should? You needn't be a "techno-geek," but you should be savvy in the use of appropriate technology.

As an example, Chris, my coauthor interviewed a prospective accountant last year, but decided against using his services when the recommended financial expert said he didn't use e-mail to communicate with clients because he hadn't figured out how to send or receive spreadsheets and data to clients.

Among my favorite "wish I hadn't said that" quotations is one by Thomas Watson, famed founder of International Business Machines, who once said, "I  think there is a world market for maybe five computers." Later, IBM became the world leader in supplying mainframe business computers, but it failed to anticipate consumer demand for personal computers. Competence in one area doesn't necessarily translate into competence in other areas. IBM abdicated its role in this market because its technical competence didn't include applying their knowledge in evolving markets. And this example is a great segué into discussing the second area of competence.

• **SYSTEMS:** More than ability to get priorities accomplished using protocols and approved systems within organizations, systems competence anticipates future trends and obstacles to success. Competence in this area requires that you know how the work flows and how to measure and assure progress toward the goal.

Teddy Roosevelt used the presidency as his "bully pulpit" while campaigning and networking to accomplish his objectives. He has been hailed as an anthropologist, writer, gamesman, and more, using his expertise in a variety of disciplines and interests to get deals done. He wrote, "Far and away the best prize that life has to offer is the chance to work hard at work worth doing." People knew that whatever he endorsed he considered worth doing. So, he wrote more letters than any other President, cutting through red tape and establishing useful relationships. He established a federal wildlife sanctuary in Florida and prepared the way for our National Parks System. These achievements never would have been possible if Roosevelt hadn't understood how governing systems are organized and how they operate.

Systems competence helps us understand why President Jimmy Carter was unable to be reelected in 1980, after he soundly defeated incumbent Gerald Ford in 1976. Carter seemed not to understand "electable" issues—how elements of the campaign system work. The voting public wasn't looking for a technically competent leader who could turn down the thermostat to 68° and wear sweaters in the White House. His election opponent, Ronald Reagan, appeared dedicated to moving forward, while Carter appeared resigned to making do. Also, Carter's team failed to capitalize on his greatest success: he brokered the Mideast Peace Agreement for which Anwar Sadat of Egypt and Menachim Begin of Israel received the Nobel Peace Prize. Carter should have shared their honor, but his team filed paperwork too late to be considered. Often, Carter's technical competence was overshadowed by systems incompetence.

As an example of how companies may not understand systems, look at Cypress Gardens, a Florida tourist attraction that closed after decades of operation. It was very different in its appeal from the many Disney-wannabe operations that blanket the central part of the state from Daytona Beach to Saint Petersburg. For decades Cypress Gardens featured beautiful strolling gardens, gentle rides, and wholesome family-oriented entertainment with water ski acrobats and magicians. My coauthor, Chris, remembers at age seven, on a Southern vacation from New York, falling in love with beautiful hostesses in hoop-skirted, antebellum fashions who strolled through the park posing for photographs. Cypress Gardens didn't seem to understand evolving tastes or marketing to new generations of tourists. Over recent years, the family-operated attraction was sold to several investors and management companies—including a brewery—that couldn't succeed in updating its appeal. New owners terminated relationships with a highly-rated religious broadcast that videotaped segments on location, and they eliminated an Easter Sunday telecast tradition enjoyed around the world. In doing so, they severed promotional ties to loyal constituents and failed to connect with new customers. They didn't understand what they had in their hands, and they didn't know how to grasp what was out of reach.

• **PEOPLE:** In addition to accomplishing objectives through high-performance teams and understanding unwritten rules of the corporate game, you must become an astute "people reader," recognizing the behavior styles, values, and motivations of others, and adapting your own style for effective interaction with them.

Lee Iococca, the Ford Motor Company executive hired to turn around Chrysler Corporation, understood how people skills impact credibility which, in turn, builds endorsement. He wrote, "A major reason capable people fail to advance is that they don't work well with their colleagues." Being able to deal successfully with superiors and subordinates is a highly prized and highly rewarded skill. Time and time again, we have seen that people's perceptions count more than our intentions. So, understanding how others see us—and how we can ensure that they see us in a positive light—is crucial to endorsement.

President Dwight Eisenhower knew that a public perception of honesty and rectitude was necessary: "The supreme quality for leadership is unquestionably integrity. Without it, no success is possible, no matter whether it is on a section gang, a football field, in an army, or in an office."

CBS News recently announced that, because of scandals sweeping through the corporate world, the prestigious Haas School of Business at the University of California at Berkeley is running background checks on prospective students. Five of 100 applicants who had been accepted to its full-time MBA program were rejected for lying on their applications. One had listed fictitious promotions, while others lied about how long  they had been out of work. All of them would have been admitted if they had told the truth, the program director said, adding that "they're really choosing to lie about things they don't need to lie about."

The applicants weren't told they'd been rejected for lying, just that they hadn't been accepted. The Wharton School of Business at the University of Pennsylvania now charges prospects $35 to have an outside firm verify their applications. What do you think? Is integrity really a people skill? It's definitely a measure of *ethical* competence, indicating an ability to trust self, others, and the reality of a situation.

Here is an interesting way that failing to understand people was part of Adam Osborne's undoing. He was a technical writer and publisher until he founded Osborne Computer Corporation in 1981, introducing the first portable personal computer. Weighing more than twenty pounds, the *Osborne 1* was hardly a laptop, but its inventor saw a future that IBM's Tom Watson failed to see. Osborne pioneered software bundling by providing word processing, spreadsheet and data base functions. That first year, Osborne sold 8,000 machines and 110,000 the next! To describe his success, one writer coined the term "hypergrowth." How then did he fail? Osborne announced that he was planning an even better model, and people stopped buying the *Osborne 1* in anticipation of the *Osborne Executive*. By the time it was released, the company was beyond salvaging.

Gaining and maintaining endorsement requires you to understand the technical, systems, and people aspects of the Competence factor.

---

2. COMMUNICATION SKILLS

• **ORAL:** Communicating concepts effectively using speech (including *skilled* speaking and listening), vocabulary, and tone of voice. It is easy for some people to intimidate verbally. Others speak impulsively, sometimes saying too much or being flippant in their responses. Controlling how you come across as you speak and listen impacts the level at which you are invited to participate.

At an annual conference of the National Speakers Association, a prospective client approached Chris Carey for assistance in working with her bosses, who were executives in an international company. Her job was to manage corporate communications, yet the men she worked for had no interest in communicating with the media, nor with stockholders, suppliers, employees, business partners, or anyone else. Basically, they had a good deal in place and saw no need to rock the boat or learn how to do more. She told Chris she hoped he could help her find a way of increasing their skills in communication so they would want to do better. He told her the process was inverted: when they wanted to do better, then they would be able to increase their skills.

• **WRITTEN:** Communicating effectively using text, including e-mail, in addition to traditional correspondence. At the university level, an educator's tenure may be connected to success in having written works published as books or articles in prestigious journals. Soon we'll see an example demonstrating how one executive's poor written communication skills almost ruined a successful company.

Under written communication skills, we can include visual appeal: how your communication looks to the reader. People who are less influenced by graphic design—color, balance, harmony, layout—tend to underestimate its value. Yet, what is your reaction to a résumé that is poorly typed? Even if all the information is accurate, won't you give more weight to one that looks more professional? How do you react to a restaurant menu that has poor-quality pictures—or worse, food stains from previous use? What does either communicate to you about the quality of food and service? If eye-appeal didn't affect credibility, food processors wouldn't spend hundreds of thousands of dollars on package designs. Publishers would release books that look like authors typed them out at their kitchen tables. If you believe your message is worthy of serious consideration, make sure to present it in ways that are aesthetically pleasing.

- **MULTIMEDIA:** Communicating effectively through means of mass communication, including news and electronic media. An early demonstration of this skill may be seen in the outcome of

---

the Nixon–Kennedy debates in 1960, in which Vice President Nixon avoided makeup and seemed ill-at-ease, while Senator Kennedy, using makeup and poise in front of the camera, impressed many viewers as responsive, even "presidential."

Today's politicians understand the value of speaking in sound bytes and appearing comfortable in the media. But everyday business people are not immune to the demands of media. At least, they must appear confident and capable in making Powerpoint-type presentations. If they fail to connect electronic images to their message because they appear incapable of using their computers, they will lose credibility with their audiences. Showing inferior high-tech skills may be as risky as not possessing these skills at all.

Is the solution to throw up your hands and admit incompetence? No. Demand for higher communication skills has created a growing market in specialists: speech writers and coaches, layout and presentation designers, along with public relations consultants are available to raise competence and increase effectiveness where technical skills are lacking.

3. USE OF FEEDBACK

- **ASKING FOR FEEDBACK** is viewed as a sign of intelligent and informed leadership. Business guru Ken Blanchard wrote that feedback is the breakfast of champions. People feel validated and included when their opinions are sought and heard.

• **RECEIVING:** Openness to suggestions and information from others, the ability to take advice and receive guidance without defensive, self-justifying behavior is seen as a sign of maturity and strength.

• **PROCESSING:** Ability to evaluate information objectively and understand its implications is a sought-after quality. This skill is knowing how to utilize the glut of data in the Information Age.

• **ACTING UPON:** Effectiveness in applying new information to bring about change and improvement is being able to turn data into action, delivering a desired outcome based on relevant incoming data.

• **REPORTING BACK:** Endorsement is given in acknowledging the value of feedback. Even if *specific* feedback isn't adopted into the operational plan, *specific* acknowledgment completes the cycle. You leave the door open for ongoing feedback when you report back sincerely, not in a disingenuous or condescending way.

4. APPEARANCE

• **EYE CONTACT:** Ability to maintain stable visual contact in conversations and negotiations, appearing neither threatening nor insecure, is a key skill. Media analysts of both political and business deals often ask, "Who blinked first?"

- **BODY LANGUAGE:** Mannerisms must agree with words. Does your body display openness and an invitation to participate, or is it closed? Do you project self-confidence that isn't threatening, or does your body-talk reveal insecurity? Even your handshake is seen as an indication of your quality and character. How do you carry yourself when you walk down the street, or when you sit at a meeting?

Yes, you can make yourself even more ill-at-ease if you fret over these factors without taking action to master them. Socrates wrote, "People believe what they see." When what you say and what people see are incongruent, people think they're seeing a mask. When those factors agree, people perceive authenticity. People may be sincere, but their "shifty" mannerisms may convey other motives. Those who thoroughly understand body language may sort out confusing messages, but amateurs may not and will read deception.

The purpose of discussing appearance is not to make you painfully self-conscious. Rather, self-awareness leads to the ability to control personal actions. Dr. Phil McGraw wrote, "If you don't acknowledge it, you can't fix it. You've got to name it to change it."

- **MANNERS:** Possessing ability to conduct yourself with civility and poise is vital. More than being polite, you demonstrate courtesy and understanding of social skills that are consistent with your position and authority, so you are seen as authoritative without being overbearing. Remember to say please and thank you.

- **DRESS:** Impressions are created by the appropriateness and style of our clothing choices. They can be used to communicate a message of authority (think of one executive's cuff links) or a message of equality (think of another executive's rolled-up shirt sleeves).

When does which style support a desired type of endorsement? What is the appropriateness of an individual's clothing choices for the occasion and for their position, not simply a "Dress for Success" mentality.

For example, Chris once saw a highly-respected image expert speak to a large assembly of cosmetic consultants. She wore a showy hat for which she is noted, but its very broad brim and the bright stage lights combined to create a shadow that made her face indistinguishable onstage. Another hat style would have been a better choice and shown that she truly understood her image in that environment. Since people believe what you do before they believe what you say, be sure your appearance delivers the right message.

5. RELATIVE POSITION

- **TITLE** implies endorsement and status by default. A certain *cachet* is attached to upper-level positions. "Professor" sounds more important than "teacher" and may be accorded more respect. Some businesses award titles in place of raises. Sensing that they are rising above peers and progressing in careers is strong motivation for some employees.

  At the same time, people who appear overly conscious of their title or position may set themselves up to be pulled down. Author C.S. Lewis wrote, "No man who says, 'I'm as good as you,' believes it. He would not say it if he did. The Saint Bernard never says it to the toy dog, nor the scholar to the dunce, nor the employable to the bum, nor the pretty woman to the plain. The claim to equality is made only by those who feel themselves to be in some way inferior. What is expressed is the itching, smarting awareness of an inferiority which the patient refuses to accept. And therefore resents." Overbearing awareness of position loses endorsement from superiors and subordinates, and both are necessary.

- **LOCATION:** Proximity and access to power is another sign of endorsement. I worked with a client  whose employee was energized when I suggested assigning her to a new office, closer to the company president, but wouldn't have been more motivated by an increase in salary. Knowing about "location endorsement" saved the company thousands of dollars in this instance and resulted in a better motivated worker.

An example of *location* endorsement may be found in an assistant who sits outside the office door of a company's senior officer. While her title might not carry much prestige, she could be the "neck" that turns the head. She may decide who gains access to the president. Ignore or abuse her at your peril!

Endorsement comes with the territory in most positional situations—most people understand title and access are not usually awarded to fools. However, *acceptance* isn't conferred by title or location; it must be *granted*.

Think about an Army Second Lieutenant recently graduated from West Point: a level of endorsement accompanies his *title,* but *acceptance* as a leader must be *granted* by the soldiers he or she commands. The troops must bestow their own endorsement by agreeing to follow this leader. As Joel Barker wrote, "A leader is someone you choose to follow to a place you would not go yourself."

Position really is relative—perhaps the governor of a small state sometimes feels less powerful than the mayor of a big city. A title conveys endorsement and status by default, but as we'll examine soon, endorsement can be lost quickly whenever the one who carries it is shown to be unworthy. With positional endorsement comes personal responsibilities.

To summarize, there are five factors that heavily influence how endorsement is given to people, organizations, and nations. They include:

- **Competence**
  - Technical
  - Systems
  - People
- **Communication Skills**
  - Oral
  - Written
  - Multimedia
- **Use of Feedback**
  - Asking for
  - Receiving
  - Processing
  - Acting upon
  - Reporting back
- **Appearance**
  - Eye contact
  - Body language
  - Manners
  - Dress
- **Relative Position**
  - Title
  - Location

CHAPTER 3:
ACHIEVING GREATER
ENDORSEMENT

When you give real endorsement to someone or something, you're putting your reputation on the line, and people know whether you're for real or simply a promoter. Endorsement comes from your heart, even though it should be validated in your head. This is the kind of endorsement you want from others, isn't it?

First, understand that acceptance and trust are not entitlements. As much as you might wish differently, these cannot be *earned*. You might feel someone *owes* them to you but, in reality, they must be *granted*. It's not your right to decide who gives you endorsement—but you can influence the outcome in your favor!

While the previous chapter listed five factors that impact endorsement, this chapter focuses on five things you can do to receive the award of greater endorsement. This is how you can win your prize.

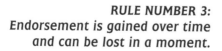

RULE NUMBER 3:
*Endorsement is gained over time
and can be lost in a moment.*

1. KNOW YOURSELF

In *First Break All the Rules,* authors Curt Kauffman and Mark Cunningham observed that self-aware people are the building blocks of great teams. Knowing and understanding yourself allows you to plot your goals and make appropriate course corrections.

17th century poet John Dryden wrote, "We first make our habits, and then our habits make us." People who truly know themselves can choose new habits and make wise choices. Others often describe them as secure in their identity and open to examining differing attitudes and beliefs.

For more than 20 years, I have advocated the use of assessment tools to help people know themselves. I recommend that my client companies assess the skills, strengths, and struggles of employees and job applicants to understand how and where they might perform best. I believe accurate assessments surpass subjective interviews in the search to know applicants and employees. I prefer assessment reports that inform those who participate as well as those who evaluate, so self-knowledge is created along with a possibility for growth and change.

 Beyond standardized intelligence, education, and skills testing, I also recommend that employers also use a behavioral style assessment, and my professional favorite utilizes the DISC Model, exploring the ways

individuals approach issues of problems, people, pace, and procedures. A background in psychology isn't required for someone to gain self-understanding when using this informative tool. Using easily understood language, it reveals the environment in which you naturally prefer to operate and measures the ways you adapt to your surroundings. The report shows your predictable responses to changes in your circumstances and how others see you in these situations. Anyone who has a desire to improve personal and professional relationships will find places to begin. Excellent resources to help you apply the DISC report information are found in my own book, *Energizing People* and in *Getting to Know You,* by my writing partner for this book, Chris Carey. (These highly-acclaimed books are available from Competitive Edge, Inc., online and by mail.)

Next, I recommend completing the Personal Interests, Attitudes and Values (PIAV) assessment to identify motivational factors that ignite passion and purpose in each individual. Some people have a strong Theoretical (learning-oriented) values system, while others are motivated by Utilitarian (function-oriented) values. Some are strongly Aesthetic (sensory-driven) and others have high Social (beneficent) motivations. Some are Traditional (conservative- or orthodox-minded) while others are Individualistic (highly independent). You'll find helpful explanations in my book, *Exploring Values: Releasing the Power of*

Attitudes, which is also available from Competitive Edge, Inc.

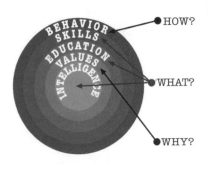

While traditional skill assessments report *what* you can do, a DISC-based report creates a profile of *how* you behave, and the PIAV report reveals the *why* behind your behaviors. These reports work hand-in-hand to provide a solid understanding of your attitudes, preferences, and actions.

Since feedback from others is helpful, a "360° profile" gathers responses from associates and provides an overview of how others view you. In many instances, I recommend that team members complete this peer-view process so they can work more cohesively. Because relatively few people understand DISC or values, they tend to judge your motivations, actions, and attitudes from a perspective you can't see. It's helpful to know the perceptions they have so you can adapt and adjust your behavior effectively.

The Scottish poet Bobby Burns wrote:

*O would some Power the gift give us
To see ourselves as others see us.*

Together, the DISC, PIAV, and 360° reports provide a rare view of ourselves with a map to self-knowledge and self-improvement. As the renowned international management expert Peter Drucker tells us, "Success in the knowledge economy comes to those who know themselves, their strengths, their values, and how they best perform."

2. CONTROL YOURSELF

Once you know your DISC behavioral style, your PIAV motivational attitudes, and understand how others see you through your 360° profile, your next step

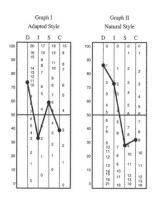

is to do something with this information. If it only provides a topic for conversation, you've missed the value of self-awareness, which is becoming more effective in your life, your work, and your relationships. In other words, apply what you know!

In the DISC *Managing for Success report,* graphs are produced that explain your natural and adapted styles. For instance, your DISC profile provides information on your natural behavioral style (Graph II) and how you adapt and adjust to succeed to your environment (Graph I). Wouldn't it make sense to integrate this information into your day-today life? Put yourself in Graph I—manage your environment and

your response to it instead of simply reacting to your surroundings, as most people do! Look at how you behave naturally and how you adapt, and then you'll see how to set yourself up for greater success—and greater endorsement!

The DISC "language" also helps you appreciate the different behavioral styles of people around you and more effectively manage your expectations for them. Combine this with an understanding of your motivational values and attitudes, and you'll know how to motivate and control yourself. In the process, you will become a better motivator of others because you'll see them more accurately. Using the feedback provided by others, you'll gain insights into how they see you, versus how you see yourself. You'll understand how important their perceptions are, and using this information, you'll move closer to gaining their trust and acceptance.

"Emotional intelligence" is a buzzword among many management and leadership experts. It refers to understanding your own hot buttons—what pushes them, who pushes them, how they are pushed and when.

 Benefits of self-knowledge and self-control are becoming more appropriate and effective in your actions and responses, your attitudes and judgments, so you stand out as someone who is in control of your

own life, who is trustworthy and capable. Someone who is deserving of endorsement.

3. KNOW OTHERS

Understanding people is a key to working with them, whether you serve in a management capacity or as a peer within a group.

Do you know what is most important to your employer, your partner, your customer, your supplier, your associate, your employee? If you don't know, how will you know where to focus in serving them? What is vital to *their* interests may be far less important to you—and vice versa! Both knowing and understanding others is a key to managing their expectations and affecting their attitudes and behavior in a positive way.

For instance, someone whose behavioral style shows a lot of "D" (Dominance) traits tends to make decisions quickly and rises to meet a challenge. After all, they operate at a fast pace and are task-oriented. On the other hand, someone who has a lot of "S" (Steadiness) traits prefers to work at a slower pace and is people-oriented. They want to take time to reach consensus and they need stability, not change. Just knowing this much, can you predict how these two individuals will work together and get along on a team if someone doesn't help them manage their differences?

Likewise, people with predominantly "I" (Influencing) traits are usually fun-loving; they are people-oriented and enthusiastic. Their behavioral preferences are very different from someone who has predominantly analytical and task-oriented "C" (Compliance) traits. One is spontaneous and the other is methodical. Yet, each is capable of making spectacular contributions to a team's success if they can work according to their style's strengths.

The DISC language allows us to interpret observable behavior without assigning our own prejudices or moral judgments to an individual's motivations and actions. Once you become skilled at observing, you can deduce their preferences for control, interaction, stability, and compliance.

You can also begin to discover their motivating values as you understand their bent toward Theoretical, Utilitarian, Aesthetic, Social, Traditional, or Individualistic attitudes.

If you could understand and relate to the behavioral styles and values preferences of your customers, associates, friends, and family, can you see how much more likely they would be to trust  you, communicate openly with you, share their real wants and needs, discuss their expectations and apprehensions? It's a fact of life that we all relate better to people we like and to people who are like us. Those are the people we lend endorsement to, as well.

I'm not promoting the power of understanding others as a method for exploiting them. Endorsement doesn't work because of manipulation, as we'll discover momentarily. When you understand people, you'll be in a better position to help them improve their performance and provide endorsement for them, because you know their struggles and strengths, their puzzles and potential, perhaps even better than they know themselves.

In today's business world, the higher you go in an organization, the more important emotional intelligence becomes and the less important technical skills become because skill with people becomes more important but much less common.

Coach Norman Van Lier said, "Once you get to the pros, coaching is not about telling people what to do; it's about managing personalities." In any high stakes business, companies can easily find supervisors to manage employee tasks—that ability is viewed as a *commodity*. But the ability to enlist the willing hearts and minds of employees is viewed as a valuable *treasure*. People who know and understand others can exercise this skill wisely, and in turn, they receive endorsement from both employers and employees.

4. DO SOMETHING FOR OTHERS

I've mentioned earlier that endorsement is reciprocal but not transactional. The best way to explain this is that true endorsement is extended without strings attached. It's not simply a "give to get" strategy where one hand washes the other. Such tactics are easily discerned because people already have their antennae up, expecting such signals. When you give from the heart, not from your head or your mouth, it's noticed and appreciated in forms of endorsement!

Here's an example, using identification with someone's difficulty. A friend of mine was checking out her purchases in a large supermarket. The cashier had obviously disconnected from her customers, because she had not greeted or even looked up at my friend as she efficiently snatched, scanned and slung items off the conveyor belt.

My friend broke the cashier's rhythm by commenting on how long the workday must have been already and the tremendous patience required to deal with irritable customers and long lines. After another comment expressing an understanding of the challenges  in such work, my friend noticed that the cashier had slowed her pace and was taking greater care in bagging the groceries. As the purchases were totaled, the cashier asked my friend if she had a coupon for one item. Upon receiving a "no" answer, she reached under the counter and handed my friend a discount coupon worth two dollars and smiled!

The cashier's demeanor changed instantly and completely because she received endorsement from my friend, by way of a sympathetic comment that recognized the value of her work and the circumstances under which she performed it. Did my friend respond to the cashier in this way because she expected a reward? No. She just knew that every person wears a sign, invisible to most, that says: *Make Me Feel Important!* By showing interest, she gave a little endorsement to the cashier, who responded by treating her with special care, opening her heart at least a little, and doing what she could to return the favor.

There are a variety of ways people understand that you endorse them, just as there are a variety of ways they acknowledge it. Some people like to be the center of attention. Their "hot button" is public recognition. Others may distrust such a show but they may appreciate a quiet nod of approval. How do you know the best way you can do something for someone else? You can start by knowing yourself and knowing others.

I recommend that you read Dr. Gary Chapman's book, *The Five Love Languages*, especially if you want to build endorsement with your spouse, your children, or others in your personal relationships. You'll find its insights apply in your professional life, too. Dr. Chapman explains that people sense others care about them and understand them when someone speaks their "love language." There are, as the book's title suggests, five love languages:

- DEEDS OF SERVICE thoughtful, without having to ask
- GIFTS and results
- WORDS that convey understanding
- TOUCH and physical attention
- TIME devoted and shared

Why is it important to understand love languages in terms of "doing something for others"? Because *how* we do something is as important as *what* we do! A classic example of how someone's love language needs can go unmet is the wife whose husband never *tells* her he loves her because words aren't important to him; he expresses care through deeds of service. Because words are important to her, she says, "You never tell me you love me when I say I love you." And he replies, "I told you I loved you when we got married 30 years ago, and if it changes, I'll let you know."

 Can you see how both husband and wife can feel a lack of endorsement and support because they don't understand each other's love language and, perhaps, even their own?

Because endorsement has reciprocal effects, one who doesn't *feel* an endorsement-worthy relationship usually doesn't *give* endorsement in return. Dr. Paul Tournier, a Swiss psychiatrist and missionary, wrote, "He who loves, understands. He who understands, loves. One who feels understood feels loved, and one who feels loved feels sure of being understood."

"But, Judy," some protest, "this isn't supposed to be a book about marriage and family. It's about endorsement!" I haven't forgotten. I use this marriage example because the easiest place to gain and lose endorsement is with those who are closest to us. Many times in teaching about behavior styles and values, I've seen people test-drive the information at home, and once they see how it works, they apply their new knowledge at work. The Endorsement Model is universal; you'll find it works everywhere.

The point is, when you do something for others, do it in terms they will understand, appreciate, and value. Do it from the heart, because people can tell the difference. Do it for them, not for yourself.

5. PROVIDE A SENSE OF CAUSAL MOTIVATION

Read the heading again. It says "causal" motivation, not "casual." This is motivation *on* purpose, *for* a purpose— instilling a sense of shared mission and common goals among people who believe their contributions count and their outcome matters.

When you set and accomplish this goal of causal motivation, you'll make it easier for workers to give endorsement to their projects, their teammates, and their leaders. They will develop a singular focus and engage obstacles to their success more creatively and optimistically. Their unity of purpose will encourage endorsement from others—sometimes from unexpected sources whose influence will help them succeed. Remember, when organizations have endorsement, they will automatically be provided the resources necessary to maintain or improve their *growth*.

It's not an accident when people come together for a common cause and achieve their purposes. You can create this effect by applying endorsement principles. As a consultant who specializes in predicting behavior, I demonstrate daily to clients that these concepts work.

Here are some key ingredients in causal motivation. The Gallup Organization surveyed more than 100,000 employees in a dozen industries. Their focus was identifying what factors workers believed were the most significant contributors in creating productive workplaces. Respondents listed these twelve factors:

• I know what is expected of me in my job.

- My work provides the opportunity to do what I do best every day.
- A supervisor or coworker cares about me as a person.
- My company's mission or purpose makes me feel the work I do is important.
- Someone at work encourages my professional development.
- The materials and equipment I need to do my work right are provided to me.
- In the past week, I've received recognition or praise for doing good work.
- My opinions count at work.
- My coworkers are committed to quality in the work we do.
- I have a best friend at work.
- I had opportunities to learn and to grow at work in the last year.
- In the last 6 months, someone at my job has talked with me about my progress.

Did you notice how many factors on this list relate directly to endorsement—that workers are validated personally and professionally? Their work matters. They are included and respected on a team. They sense progress and a future in their careers. They can excel. Think about this in terms of employee success beyond your own endorsement.

There is also a demonstrable connection between these 12 worker beliefs and a company's profitability, productivity, employee loyalty, and customer satisfaction. When Gallup ranked the businesses that supported these 12 beliefs, the top 25% of companies averaged 14% higher revenues and 10% lower employment turnovers than the rest of the companies! Do you see how these results can create increasingly higher levels of endorsement, generosity, confidence, and trust beyond the norm?

Remember, though, that Rule #3 says: Endorsement is gained over time and can be lost in an moment. A thoughtless comment or reckless attitude can undo relationships where endorsement, generosity, confidence, and trust have been the norm. We'll devote a chapter to loss of endorsement and what can be done when it happens. It's sometimes possible to recover a level of endorsement, but as you'll see, it's better to work to keep it than to work to regain it.

Develop habits that support endorsement:
- **Know yourself.**
- **Control yourself.**
- **Know others.**
- **Do something for others.**
- **Provide a sense of causal motivation and shared mission.**

CHAPTER 4:
THE LAW OF RECIPROCITY

The "Law of Reciprocity" greases the gears and makes everything work more smoothly. Advanced by the fathers of contingency theory, Paul Lawrence and Jay Lorsch in their book, *Organization and Development,* reciprocity explains that when people feel or know they have endorsement, they will give back in terms of *performance.*

According to studies, in most developed countries, people can work at 70 percent of their capability without losing their jobs. On an academic scale, that is C-minus work. Without benefit of endorsement, the *best* performance most workers give is 80 percent. Although that sounds better, it is only C-plus work.

Do you recall the work of the Italian economist Vilfredo Pareto, who formulated what's commonly known as the "80/20 Rule"? He discovered that 80 percent of the land in his country was con-

RULE #4:
When people have
endorsement, they give
back through improved
performance.

---

trolled by 20 percent of the population.

Many people think of the 80/20 Rule as a principle in life:

- In sales, 80 percent of your income is provided by 20 percent of your customers, while 80 percent of your customers provide the other 20 percent of the money.
- In the publishing business, 80 percent of new books share only 20 percent of the marketing money, while those thought to be in the top 20 percent divide 80 percent of promotional funds.
- In classrooms, 80 percent of a teacher's disciplinary incidents trace to 20 percent of the students, and the remaining 20 percent of incidents occur among the other 80 percent of students.

The list of incidents where this appears to be true seems infinite. On the previous page, the statistics on job performance remind me of the 80/20 Rule: without endorsement, most workers operate at 80 percent or less of their capacity while far fewer workers operate at maximum capacity (approaching 100 percent). Endorsement is key in improved performance.

When employees *feel* they have received endorsement, they perform at maximum capacity.

You can't create endorsement just by devoting twenty minutes each day to saying nice things to other people. Instead, establish a climate in which trust, communication, genuineness, accountability, care, and cooperation can flourish.

In his book *Getting to Know You,* Chris Carey, wrote a chapter entitled "Finesse is Stronger than Force." He used an analogy in which a hammer pounding on a screw represented the *force* some people exert roughly to get their way. A screwdriver twisting in the screw represented the *finesse* that can get the job done smoothly with minimal fuss and effort. In a hostile work environment, order is maintained by *enforcing compliance* instead of *encouraging cooperation.* Using threats of termination or demotion to hammer out results reminds me of the office memo: "Firings will continue until morale improves!"

Companies that fail to understand emotional intelligence emphasize order and control instead. They expend great amounts of energy to gain compliance, then waste even more to sustain and enforce it. Resentment builds among those they control because power plays have that effect.

You may be wondering in what other ways people can be motivated without using threats to control them or money to induce them. Here are five methods to consider:

- Let them work their own schedules.
- Give them plum assignments.
- Find advancement opportunities for them.
- Praise them in front of their peers.
- Keep your promises.

This isn't a new millennium management concept—it's actually an old one. Johann Wolfgang von Goethe taught it early in the 19th century, although it is thousands of years older than his words: "If we take people as we find them, we may make them worse, but if we treat them as though they are what they should be, we help them to become what they are capable of becoming." A good part of the reason this works is that people reciprocate our endorsement by improving their performance.

Okay, if you insist on a more modern management source, consider Gary Markle's words in his business management book, *Catalytic Coaching:* "Few aspects of a supervisor position are as personally satisfying as helping someone once thought of as a poor performer redefine herself in a positive light. There is a great deal of satisfaction that comes from knowing you were a critical catalyst in an employee's successful effort to grow, develop, and win."

Coach Lou Holtz said, "When you bring a group of people together, it's called a *start.* When you get a group of people to stay together, it's called *progress.* When you get a group of people to work together, it's called *success.*"

Benjamin Franklin suggested that when we are forthright in acknowledging our own mistakes and our desire to do better, people go out of there way to reciprocate: "Years have taught me at least one thing and that is not to try to avoid an unpleasant fact, but rather to grasp it firmly and let the other person observe that I am at least treating him fairly. Then he, it has been my observation, will treat me in the same spirit."

Jack Welch, the retired head of General Electric, wrote, "Make people believe what they think and do is important, and then get out of the way while they do it." Why? Because when you give people this level of endorsement, they'll run over you getting it done and fulfilling your trust.

Do you know why I just quoted these respected authorities to get my point across? Endorsement, of course! If you don't respect my opinion, you might be open to theirs. If you won't believe me, you should believe them. And if I use words from people you trust, you tend to reciprocate by extend-ing some trust to me.

In fact, an unknown writer of past days claimed, "people will ac-cept your ideas much more readily

if you tell them that Benjamin Franklin said it first."
As you can see, endorsement works as a bridge
from what is proven to what is still being proved.

There is a predictable payoff to the way we treat
people: a study of 7,500 employees, conducted by
Watson Wyatt Worldwide, revealed that only half
of the workers trusted their senior managers. The
same survey also showed that shareholder returns
were 42 percentage points higher when employees
trusted their top executives.

What are you doing to build trust? It's not about
corporate programs as much as personal commitment. In the 18th century, Samuel Johnson wrote,
"He who waits to do a great deal of good at once
will never do anything. Life is made up of little
things. True greatness consists in being great in
little things." You can start now, where you are.

Here are two examples from the airline indus-
try that demonstrate the Law of Reciprocity in high
gear: In the 1980s, Delta Air Lines employees purchased a Boeing 727 airplane in celebration of their
company's birthday. The word "family" described
Delta's business culture in those days. And, after
the September 11th tragedies in 2001,
many airlines endured huge layoffs and
suffered large financial losses, but
Southwest Airlines' employees volunteered for pay cuts and the

company was able to avoid laying off any workers. Both instances show that employees endorsed their companies and their coworkers—they were all in it together! They shared a mission and a causal motivation, and they invested in each other.

In another example, a shirt factory, located in New England, burned down. The relationship between the owner and his employees was so solid that the owner continued to pay his employees while the factory was being rebuilt. Why? Obviously, he believed the company's future lay with his employees.

So how do businesses earn such loyalty from employees? As the saying goes, "Success isn't purchased at any one time, but on the installment plan."

Management guru Ken Blanchard wrote, "Managers have two choices: hire winners or develop them." As much as I am an advocate for assessing workers' skills, behaviors, and attitudes to make the best hiring decisions, I believe Blanchard is correct. Employers must do more than assess; they must apply. The examples just cited show that developing winners, rather than just hiring workers, pays unexpected dividends.

By now you've figured out that the ripple effects of endorsement provide a better result. Remember:

- **Rule #4: When people have endorsement, they give back through improved performance.** Remember the Gallup survey results that showed how the top 25 percent of companies that supported the twelve key employee beliefs averaged 14 percent higher revenues and 10 percent lower employee turnovers than the rest of the companies surveyed.

- **Rule #3: Endorsement is gained over time and can be lost in a moment.** Practice emotional intelligence in your responses to others. It will allow you to gain—and retain—endorsement.

- **Rule #2: Performance is directly proportional to endorsement.** To raise performance, provide endorsement cautiously, but when it is deserved, give it generously.

- **Rule #1: Endorsement is dynamic, not static.** Understand that you must make deposits into endorsement accounts if you plan to make withdrawals. Continue lifelong learning and practice endorsement even after you think you understand it.

CHAPTER 5:
LOSS OF ENDORSEMENT

The field of politics has become a graveyard for those who used their public favor callously or carelessly:

- Lyndon Johnson beat Barry Goldwater in the Presidential Election of 1964 by the largest margin to date. Yet his leadership in the Vietnam era became so unpopular that he decided not to run for reelection in 1968.

- In 1972, President Richard Nixon was elected to his second term by an even larger margin, as his opponent carried only his own home state. Two years later, Nixon left office in shame and humiliation as his administration's betrayal of the public trust split the nation.

- Jimmy Carter, hands-down winner of the next Presidential election, lost to Ronald Reagan by large numbers in the following one and is remembered more for his achievements after leaving the presidency. Carter was in no sense a Washington insider—in fact,

RULE #5:
Favor and influence are fickle.

that worked for him in his election campaign and against his administration. He developed a reputation as a micro- manager, which was not a popular trait among staffers and bureaucrats.

Historically, past presidents have faded into the background, having deemed their public service the extent of their duty to others. I enjoy mentioning the accomplishments of President Carter's "second career" because he is one of the best examples of regaining endorsement. Today, he is widely regarded for his work with Habitat for Humanity and is an honored recipient of the Nobel Peace Prize. So, if you are struggling over Loss of Endorsement, know that there is hope for you, too.

The following two pages represent a major tactical blunder by the CEO of a $1.5 billion healthcare software company. Neal Patterson was cofounder of Cerner Corporation and recently elevated to company president when he launched an impulsive e-mail to the organization's 400 Kansas City-based managers in March, 2001. He did unexpected harm to employee morale and his rapport with managers, to stockholder goodwill and his reputation in the business community—and lost $28 million dollars personally, as the company's stock plummeted 22% in only three days! Amazingly, all this happened just before the company was to be named by *Fortune* magazine as one of the 100 Best Companies to work for in America! Here is Patterson's note:

```
From:        Patterson,Neal
To:          DL_ALL_MANAGERS;
Subject:     MANAGEMENT DIRECTIVE:  Week #10_01:
             Fix it or changes will be made
Importance:  High
```

==========

To the KC_based managers:

I have gone over the top. I have been making this point for over one year. We are getting less than 40 hours of work from a large number of our KC-based EMPLOYEES. The parking lot is sparsely used at 8AM; likewise at 5PM. As managers -- you either do not know what your EMPLOYEES are doing; or YOU do not CARE. You have created expectations on the work effort which allowed this to happen inside Cerner, creating a very unhealthy environment. In either case, you have a problem and you will fix it or I will replace you.

NEVER in my career have I allowed a team which worked for me to think they had a 40 hour job. I have allowed YOU to create a culture which is permitting this. NO LONGER.

At the end of next week, I am plan to implement the following:
1. Closing of Associate Center to EMPLOYEES from 7:30AM to 6:30PM.
2. Implementing a hiring freeze for all KC based positions. It will require Cabinet approval to hire someone into a KC based team. I chair our Cabinet.
3. Implementing a time clock system, requiring EMPLOYEES to 'punch in' and 'punch out' to work. Any unapproved absences will be charged to the EMPLOYEES vacation.
4. We passed a Stock Purchase Program, allowing for the EMPLOYEE to purchase Cerner stock at a 15% discount, at Friday's BOD meeting. Hell will freeze over before this CEO implements ANOTHER EMPLOYEE benefit in this Culture.
5. Implement a 5% reduction of staff in KC.
6. I am tabling the promotions until I am convinced that the ones being promoted are the solution, not the problem. If you are the problem, pack you bags.

I think this parental type action SUCKS. However, what you are doing, as managers, with this company makes me SICK. It makes sick to have to write this directive.

I know I am painting with a broad brush and the majority of the KC based associates are hard working, committed to Cerner success and committed to transforming health care. I know the parking lot is not a great measurement for 'effort'. I know that 'results' is what counts, not 'effort'. But I am through with the debate. We have a big vision. It will require a big effort. Too many in KC are not making the effort.

I want to hear from you. If you think I am wrong with any of this, please state your case. If you have some ideas on how to fix this problem, let me hear those. I am very curious how you think we got here. If you know team members who are the problem, let me know. Please include (copy) Kynda in all of your replies.

I STRONGLY suggest that you call some 7AM, 6PM and Saturday AM team meetings with the EMPLOYEES who work directly for you. Discuss this serious issue with your team. I suggest that you call your first meeting -- tonight. Something is going to change.

I am giving you two weeks to fix this. My measurement will be the parking lot: it should be substantially full at 7:30 AM and 6:30 PM. The pizza man should show up at 7:30 PM to feed the starving teams working late. The lot should be half full on Saturday mornings. We have a lot of work to do. If you do not have enough to keep your teams busy, let me know immediately.

Folks this is a management problem, not an EMPLOYEE problem. Congratulations, you are management. You have the responsibility for our EMPLOYEES. I will hold you accountable. You have allowed this to get to this state. You have two weeks. Tick, tock.

Neal ….
Chairman & Chief Executive Officer
Cerner Corporation www.cerner.com
"We Make Health Care Smarter"

How did Neal Patterson's e-mail message become public, cause all that damage, and ultimately become a textbook example of how *not* to handle employee relations? Simple: a disgruntled manager posted the note on a Yahoo.com website frequented by investors, and word spread quickly. The story appeared in *Forbes* and *Fortune* magazines, and in business newspapers like the *Financial Times* and *The Wall Street Journal*.

What did Cerner and Patterson do to control the damage? The corporation handles its P.R. internally, according to Mainsail.com. As this chapter is being written, the company's website, www.cerner.com, has not acknowledged or addressed the issue, nor has the company issued an official retraction beyond quotes from their CEO in various news articles.

Patterson's media comments weren't very apologetic, as he acknowledged that his "direct language" had offended some people: "To this group, I sincerely apologize to you if I offended you." He told Kansas City *Star* reporters, "There are a lot of people trying to make this negative... Do I regret it? I'd hate to change." He saw his blunt style of management as evidence of a plainspoken country upbringing, adding that you could take the boy off the farm but not take the farm out of the boy. "I was trying to start a fire," he said. "I lit a match, and I started a firestorm."

Rereading his memo, you'll notice some carelessness in Patterson's grammar and spelling. But you'll see deliberate phrasing as well. For instance, until this time, workers at Cerner were always referred to as associates, not as employees. It was part of an intentional business culture to let them know how much their contributions were valued and respected. To refer to them as employees—in capital letters—was an insult to them.

Adding injury to insult, he froze promotions, threatened to close the employee gym, install time clocks—and provided a hard-to-measure standard of progress: that the parking lot's 1,900 spaces be half-filled at odd hours.

According to Patterson, he typed a draft of his message early in the morning, then met with a client, then had two managers and his assistant read over the memo, and then sent it just before noon. So it appears he may have had several opportunities to rethink his communication plan.

A variety of business pundits have suggested ways this mess could have been handled beyond the obvious: that Patterson never should have hit "send." According to their wisdom, Cerner (the company) and Patterson (the leader) could have:

• issued a formal apology as soon as they realized the memo had been leaked to the outside world.

- posted responses to the postings in every Internet news forum where the message was posted.

- taken action to communicate with investors before analysts began speculating on the company's future.

Mainsail.com had an interesting P.R. suggestion: Cerner could have turned lemons into lemonade by lampooning the memo, making a video featuring Patterson, standing in the deserted company parking lot, dispensing donuts and coffee to employees who showed up early! Mainsail acknowledges that attempting to defuse the situation with humor might have seemed to trivialize its seriousness, but it might not have been worse than doing nothing at all.

Before we move to other examples of losing endorsement, this is a good place to recall a story about Abraham Lincoln. Having received a letter hotly criticizing his fitness to be President, he sat down at his desk and wrote a lengthy response. When he finished his reply, it's said that Lincoln tore it into pieces and tossed it in the trash. His wife asked him why he had done such an unusual thing, and Lincoln replied, "I needed to write it but he didn't need to read it."

A sad reality in losing endorsement is that people remember failures more readily than successes. Jack Welch, the CEO of General Electric, retired from the company as a living legend. His autobiography describing his business successes became a New York *Times* best-seller.

But Welch's personal exploits overshadowed his professional achievements when it was discovered that the married executive had a romantic liaison with the female editor of the *Harvard Business Review*. As details came to light, the editor left her job, and Jane Beasley Welch filed for divorce after 13 years of marriage. As the Welches fought over marital assets, details began to emerge that reflected badly on the company, its former leader, and its board of directors.

Mrs. Welch contends that GE covered enormous living costs for them while Mr. Welch led the company—and will continue to do so for him for the rest of his life. Trouble is, the extent of benefits had never been disclosed publicly, and no one seems to understand all its ramifications.

The company's official statement says Welch remains a consultant to the company on a retainer of $86,000 a year and continues to have access to GE services and facilities. Mrs. Welch claims this includes corporate aircraft, use of a GE-owned luxury apartment on Central Park West, floor-level seats to the New York Knicks, courtside seats at the U.S. Open, membership in private clubs—even satellite TV at his homes in Connecticut, Massachusetts, and Florida, plus all the costs associated with the New York apartment, from wine and food to laundry, toiletries and newspapers.

The deal was struck in 1996, to keep Welch at GE until his 65th birthday. It entitles him to every benefit as a retiree and consultant that was his as an employee. His $86,000 annual salary actually covers his first 30 days of work, with $17,000 for each additional day. Records indicate the company also pays his life insurance premiums and a $9 million annual pension.

General Electric's stock fell amid concerns about the economy and its lack of financial transparency. Aggravating the situation is the knowledge that Welch's stock alone is worth more than $900 million, and his retirement package is irrevocable. Graef Crystal, a specialist in corporate pay, said, "This is an indictment of GE's board of directors. This is the most appalling use of corporate assets. No one had any idea of the magnitude of what the company had been giving him." Crystal said either the board didn't know about it or was asleep at the switch.

None of this information was volunteered by GE. "It is appalling to me that Jack Welch's flowers are being paid for by retired firemen and teachers who are the GE shareholders and don't know this is going on," said Nell Minow, editor of *The Corporate Library,* quoted in the Atlanta *Journal-Constitution.* "The reason executive compensation and employment contracts are disclosed is so investors know whether the interests of executives are aligned with those of shareholders and whether the board is doing its job." Based on publicly available information, shareholders don't know.

Do you understand that we're focusing on loss of endorsement, not on whether Jack Welch deserves his compensation package? From an outsider's view, it seems everything unraveled at a personal level and then ripples spread into the professional—extending even to the Augusta National golf tournament, in Georgia. When it was revealed that GE paid for executive memberships in this male-only private club, protests were unleashed that the company supported glass ceilings that limit career progress for female executives. In addition to undermining confidence among some women employees, GE also lost endorsement with some stockholders. And it raised questions about its own commitment to gender equality, even after they spent millions on diversity training and compliance programs.

The point is this: whenever endorsement is gained or lost, there is a ripple effect. Lost endorsement doesn't make gentle ripples, though—it creates waves that sometimes swamp every boat that's in the water. Allow these experiences to inspire you to keep your endorsement high...and dry!

Before we leave Loss of Endorsement, let's look briefly at steps to restoring it. First, understand that a phenomenon similar to the Pareto Effect is at work when you want to establish approval and credibility with others. This bell-curve signifies the population's readiness to accept you.

NO   MAYBE   YES

At the left, you can see some percentage of people who will always respond negatively to you, no matter what you do. Their reaction is not because of something you have done; it's because they have a prejudice that imposes itself on you. Perhaps they distrust every man with a beard or moustache, and you fit that description—surprisingly, up to 30 percent of the population has this prejudice! Or, your mannerisms may remind them of someone they disliked in elementary school. Your name may sound similar to a boss who fired them years ago. Any number of nonsense reasons may account for someone's prejudgment of you. You'll never win their approval, so endorsement is unlikely. It's as if they like only peanut butter cookies and you are selling chocolate chips. Just live with the understanding that your cookies are okay anyway. Assuming you look presentable and don't blatantly violate a basic rule of conduct or hygiene, sales trainers say this percentage should be less than 10 percent.

If this sounds like bad news, you'll be

pleased to hear the good news: at the other end of the bell-curve, a similar percentage of people will accept you, like you, and even endorse you for no particular reason. This may mean they are as indiscriminate as the other extreme is discriminating. It's tempting to think they like us because of our character or good looks, but the probable truth is that we remind them of an old friend, or a character in a story— or a favorite uncle who had a moustache, too. While it would seem a person can use all the friends she can get, someone who relates to you so positively for no reason is probably just as impulsive in forming other relationships. It's not that you must avoid these people, just understand that they'll like the next person who comes along just as much.

The good news is found in the large segment that lies between the two extremes. At least 80 percent of the people you meet have no preformed opinion of you and tend to suspend judgment until they can find out more about you. It is with these people that your endorsement-building skills matter most.

How can you know where people will fall in your bell-curve? Meet them and find out! Your knowledge of behavioral styles and motivational attitudes will help you build rapport more quickly with more people. Your understanding of what goes into establishing credibility and influence will serve you well in giving and gaining influence, but remember that endorsement is always a choice, never a right. Regardless of how you are treated by people at any point on your bell-curve, adopt this standard from William Lyon Phelps: "This is the final test of a gentleman: his respect for those who can be of no possible value to him."

Do you want to regain endorsement? It's not always possible, because endorsement—an expression of trust—is not *earned*; it is *granted*. But whatever the outcome, you honor others in your sincere efforts to restore what has been lost.

Your first step is honesty, and your second is humility. Ralph Waldo Emerson wrote, "Whatever games are played with us, we must play no games with ourselves, but deal in our privacy with the last honesty and truth." Tell yourself the truth. It may take time to come to terms with yourself and your failure. It's true, as Zig Ziglar says, that failure is an *event*, not a *person*. Even the gravest downfall is not permanent if you can find the courage to pick yourself up, dust yourself off, and start again.

Gaining endorsement isn't about hustling people, and restoring endorsement isn't about negotiating favor. When you've blown it, whether through negligence, ignorance, stupidity, or chance, the first thing to do is admit your own your mistake. Identify your real offense (if you don't already know). It may take time to understand its real scope and impact. Don't make restoring trust your goal. Instead, make integrity your aim. Albert Einstein said, "Try not to become a person of success but rather to become a person of value."

Humility enters the picture when you apologize or work to make amends. Anyone who has been affected by your actions will have "radar" up to detect insincerity, falsehood, or manipulation. People will even read it where it isn't present because of their desire for self-protection. It's important that your conversations not become excuses for your behavior, and whenever possible, they should be specific and to the point. "Sorry about that" apologies don't address the reasons behind loss of endorsement.

At the same time, your circle of confession need not be larger than the circle of offense. You owe no explanation to the merely curious but you may to those involved. Often it is wise to confide in a few true friends who understand and will help you face your situation honestly, humbly, and courageously. At other times, you should confide details only to an attorney. You may also want to discuss your actions with a spiritual advisor.

Business developer Scott Michael said, "People of integrity expect to be believed. When they are not, they let time prove them right." If you're for real, time is on your side because it will verify your true motives and intentions. Time never operates in reverse, so you must live from this moment forward with thoughts of forgiveness for your past, hope for your future, and responsibility for today.

You'll want to put into place a system that helps you avoid repeat offenses. "Accountability" isn't a popular idea, but those who want to climb to the top and stay there understand the importance of building into their lives people who will encourage them to be their best and do their best. Chris calls them "people who can tell you no and make it stick," not because they have power over you but because you have granted them authority to help you succeed in life.

A corporate blueprint for regaining endorsement is plainly seen in the Extra-Strength Tylenol cyanide-poisoning case of 1982. Although Johnson & Johnson and its subsidiary, McNeil Consumer Products, were innocent of any wrongdoing, they acted quickly to protect the public instead of themselves when 7 people suddenly died in Chicago after using the medication. They used the media effectively to warn against consuming any Tylenol product, cooperated fully with authorities at every opportunity where they could have stonewalled, and recalled 31 million Tylenol capsules at a cost of over $100 million. An Internet search will yield the whole story quickly, an enviable example of how business should be done. Along with it, you'll find comparisons of how Perrier handled benzene-tainted drinking water. That episode is a text-book example of how *not* to handle a problem. As I said earlier, people remember failures more readily than successes. Zig warns us: "Discipline weighs *ounces*; regret, *tons*." Learn to carry a light load.

Here is a summary of our lessons on the loss of endorsement, remember that:

- **Remember Rule #5: Favor and influence are fickle.**
- **Just because you need to say something is no reason someone else has to hear it.**
- **Be proactive in addressing failure.**
- **Understand that not everybody likes chocolate chips.**
- **Choose honesty and humility to make amends.**
- **Time is on your side if you're for real.**
- **Be accountable to people who want to see you succeed.**

CHAPTER 6: YOUR ENDORSEMENT QUOTIENT

In this closing chapter, we're going to look at "endorsement on purpose," including ways to measure and improve your own ability to gain and give endorsement through positive influence.

Does the expression "we've always done it that way" ring any bells? The following information illustrates both unexpected influence and unintended consequences.

The U.S. Standard railroad gauge—the distance between the rails—is exactly 4 feet, 8½ inches. Why was this gauge chosen? Because it's the track width familiar to English expatriates who designed and built the earliest U.S. railroads.

England's rail lines were constructed by workers who built the pre-railroad tramways, using the same jigs and tools to line up with the wheel ruts in many of the old long distance roads that crisscross England.

RULE #6:
Perceptions differ from realities in ourselves and in others.

Imperial Rome gets credit for the first of those old rutted roads that became the standard for all of Europe. Roman war chariots, accompanying invading armies, formed the initial ruts. Every chariot was identical in specifications, requiring that each be built just wide enough to accommodate the back ends of two war horses. Centuries later, wagon builders gauged their wheels to match so they wouldn't be destroyed by the ruts.

So the United States Standard railroad gauge of 4 feet, $8^1/2$ inches is actually derived from the original government specifications for an Imperial Roman war chariot. Bureaucracies live forever!

Now here's an interesting update to this story:

When we see an assembled NASA Space Shuttle sitting on its Florida launch pad, two big booster rockets are attached to the sides of its main fuel tank. These are solid rocket boosters, or SRBs, made by Morton-Thiokol at their factory in Utah.

The engineers who designed the SRBs might have preferred to make them fatter, but the rockets must be shipped by train from the factory to the launch site. At times, railroad lines between the two sites run through tunnels carved in mountains— some of which are only slightly wider than the railroad tracks they ride on. Of course, those railroad tracks conform to the U.S. Standard railroad gauge of ex-

actly 4 feet, 8¹/₂ inches. Following the chain of events back to ancient Rome, you can see that a major design feature of the world's most advanced transportation system was actually determined over two thousand years ago...by the width of a horse's butt.

Did you get the point? The lifespan of your influence can be much longer than you think. You needn't be well-known or important to make a difference—an obscure chariot builder thousands of years ago still influences the size of space rockets today. The ripple effect of your decisions may have unexpected influence and unintended consequences over time.

How can someone like you become a powerful influence in *today's* culture? According to Ed Keller and Jon Berry, authors of The *Influentials*, influence comes as a by-product of savvy and trust.

Keller is CEO of RoperASW, a global marketing research company. Over several decades, he has watched the evolution of what he calls "the persuasive 10 percent" as a barometer of public tastes. According to his book, the decisions made by 90 percent of consumers—including our choices of cars, restaurants, personal computers, and financial institutions—are influenced by the other 10 percent.

"From big-ticket to small-ticket items, to everyday issues and problems, consumers are turning to word-of-mouth from people they know, and it's these one in 10 Americans who have become the trusted, turned-to people," Keller told a reporter for the Atlanta *Journal-Constitution.*

Keller and Berry say consumers are less trusting of traditional institutions to influence their choices, such as advertising, government, media, employers, and major brand names. This leaves a void in the marketplace that is increasingly being filled by the opinions of people they call "Influentials."

Self-reliance has replaced trust in the marketplace. This translates into more people turning to other people for advice and information on everything from vacations to must-see movies.

For his part, Jon Berry, RoperASW's vice president and senior director of research, has developed revealing profiles of typical Influentials. They are men and women, median age 45, with a college background, married with children, homeowners, with secure, good-paying jobs. More than the general public, their interests include reading newspapers, magazines and books, traveling, cooking, exercising, spending time online, attending cultural events, volunteering in the community, and enjoying music. Often, they are local activists who organize petitions, run church groups, raise funds for the library, and write letters to the editor.

How does this group gain such influence? According to Keller, it's because they invest their time. They believe individuals can make a difference. They have a reputation for getting things done. And in that respect they have earned the trust of their friends and neighbors.

Their influence over products—what the rest of us see in the stores—is because they tend to be more outspoken, more willing to experiment and adopt new ideas. Consumer trends move from niche markets, through status-oriented buyers, and finally into the mainstream. Influentials are on the leading edge of these trends, and they return products they don't like.

Influentials's current interests determine what's hot and what's not. Broadband, digital photography, MP3 players storing thousands of songs, and DVD players are examples of products that came to prominence after being adopted first by Influentials. Berry said, "You see them start to talk about things, and then you start to see those things surfacing."

We're not talking about *trendiness*. We're looking at the origin of actual trends, and true Influentials aren't easily caught up in hype. Marketers are learning what makes Influentials tick and then targeting their buying interests. As an example, Amazon.com had planned a $50-million-a-year television ad campaign, but they switched their focus to services that could be publicized by word-of-mouth, such as free shipping on larger purchases. This program was very effective in recruiting new customers and rewarding increased purchases because people talked it up.

Influentials are proactive. According to RoperASW research, 40 percent of Influentials have unresolved complaints about a product or service. They e-mail customer-service sites to offer both criticisms and suggestions. In the old days, when customer feedback was less accessible and less direct, marketers and manufacturers were hard-pressed to find the candid responses offered by these consumers. Their willingness to speak up and stand out is what makes them influential.

Businesses understand that complaints from their most influential consumers can't be treated as nuisances anymore, because, Keller says, "if they treat them wrong, that will multiply, And if they treat them right, that will multiply." As we considered earlier in Chapter 3, the way feedback is received, accepted, encouraged, and responded to impacts credibility and endorsement for individuals, companies, and nations. Influentials win the right to be heard, and when they do that responsibly, their influence matters.

Oprah Winfrey used endorsement and media savvy to create Oprah's Book Club, the literary seal of approval for millions of her fans, and she has put many books on the bestseller list. Dr. Phil McGraw, Tiger Woods, and other celebrities have used their public endorsement profitably for commercial influence.

Personal credibility and personal influence are at the core of effective referral-based and network-marketing programs, too. Think about this: people recommend their favorite restaurants, stores, products, movies, travel services—even their children's orthodontists and more—every day to friends and strangers. Influence makes referrals work. While businesses benefit from their positive word-of-mouth, there wasn't a way for "regular folks" to profit from the influence of their referral activities before network marketing. Of course, as with any other product or service, if the person making the referral turns out to be unreliable or untrustworthy, or if the product or service is deficient, then few people will continue to trust or show interest in such programs.

Some people in network marketing overemphasize the quality of their product in hopes of advancing their success. Truthfully, much of their success will depend on their ability to establish personal and professional credibility. I'm not saying quality products are not necessary; they are. But quality leadership is necessary, too. Of the many opportunities that are available to prospective distributors, most who succeed in multilevel or network marketing programs are connected to an upline they trust and respect, someone to whom they give (and from whom they receive) endorsement. Such companies are judged by the quality of their leadership and the quality of distributors

---

those leaders attract. The principles of endorsement taught in this book will prove themselves to any network marketer who applies them consistently.

Here is a tactic that dilutes influence: In his book, *The 7 Habits of Highly Effective People,* Dr. Stephen Covey discusses "circles of influence" and "circles of concern." He points out that some people waste their efforts by trying to fix circumstances over which they have no real influence, only concern.

If you have ever been in this position, you know that you can become frustrated when you don't see results. Some people become more aggressive in a bid to achieve their purpose, but without influence and endorsement, they may only spin their wheels and alienate others. Some people obsess about what they can't accomplish, while others give up and find another out-of-reach concern to work on.

Wherever your personal endorsement is weak, your circle of influence is small. Wanting to accomplish more, you can be distracted from what you can do by all the things that concern you. You may find it easy to march in a parade for Save the Whales yet be unable to actually do anything for the puppies being put to sleep down at the dog pound. This is what Covey means about working on our concerns—things out of reach—instead of in our circle of influence, where we can have direct impact.

This illustration shows that there are many issues you are concerned about but fewer issues you directly influence. Covey says that, as you improve your effectiveness in the areas where you can influence outcomes, your credibility will increase (shown as expanding circles) to encompass more and more of your concerns. In effect, your influence may grow to include them.

Endorsement is effective within the endorser's circle of influence. For instance, if someone you know and like shares a common interest with you, this individual's positive recommendation on that subject will carry weight with you. But if someone you don't know or respect offers a similar opinion, you won't be as positively influenced by their comments. On the other hand, your good friends' endorsing comments about subjects in which they have no experience won't have the same influence as would some experts.

Now that you understand how the Model of Endorsement operates, you can see why your own influence, coupled with the influence of others, is vital to success. Again, one reason many people are not effective where they wish to be is because they are failing to be effective where they already are.

We've written this book to help you become an *intentional* (instead of an accidental) influence. As you use these principles you will gain endorsement from people who support your goals and align their strengths with yours. In addition, you will become a "key player," able to provide your own endorsement to assist worthy individuals, organizations, companies, and projects.

How are you doing as a gainer and giver of endorsement? As I consult with companies, it always proves helpful to measure their growth and impact in the endorsement process. If this study has been just an interesting exercise for you, then it has missed its target. Its goal is to change your ability to lead a life of high impact and influence!

You'll do well to cultivate habits that lead to endorsement, and you can start with the self-assessment questions on the following page. Your responses will be only as helpful as you are honest. You can make up answers that sound more favorable, but you'll benefit from telling yourself the truth. And don't make this a onetime thing. Copy the next page so you can ask yourself at least 3 of the 5 questions every week as you develop the habit of thinking this way automatically.

ENDORSEMENT QUESTIONS

1. What have I done to gain endorsement this week? _____

_____

_____

2. How have I given endorsement to someone else recently? _____

_____

_____

3. What have I done to lose endorsement in the last week? _____

_____

_____

4. How was I given endorsement by someone last week? _____

_____

_____

5. What impact did giving, receiving, or losing endorsement have on my performance or the performance of others? _____

_____

_____

6. At least once a month, ask your boss or other people in your life what you can do to increase your endorsement.

Think how such a feedback process might work in your career, especially compared to the once-a-year performance evaluations many companies cling to. Workers can be made to feel insignificant because no one provides timely correction or encouragement. Then, once a year, someone pulls them into an office and says, "I didn't like it when you did such-and-such six months ago. In fact, it bothers me enough now that I'm going to downgrade your performance review—but it didn't bother me enough at the time that I would help you work through it. A year from now, we'll reexamine your progress, so this is fair warning: don't do such-and-such again."

When a workplace survey examined what motivates the best workers, annual performance reviews didn't even make the list, but these factors did:

WHAT MOTIVATES TOP PERFORMERS

• Desire to maintain good work reputation	81%
• Importance of their work	76%
• Appreciation of others	66%
• Opportunity to prove capability to others	57%
• Interesting work	51%

 Since annual employee appraisal is the main method many companies choose to address performance problems, is it surprising that 22 percent of responding readers told *Maxim* magazine that their supervisors could be replaced by hamsters and no one would notice? How much endorsement did the survey respondents give to their bosses? About as much as their bosses give them on an annual basis, I'll bet!

This chapter isn't about how people's job performance is evaluated. It's about how people are endorsed. A company can recruit, select, and hire the right person for the job; but statistics show when those people aren't managed correctly, they either become poor performers, have high health costs, or leave. And this is why understanding your own Endorsement Quotient is vital, whether you are the supervisor or the supervised. We all need to give and receive endorsement to be effective.

Management expert Jan Carlzon wrote, "If you manage people by love—that is, if you show them respect and trust—they perform up to their real capabilities." In other words, giving and gaining endorsement makes a measurable difference. As we saw on the previous page, endorsement imparts a good reputation, which motivates 81 percent of top-performing employees. Reinforcing the importance of their work motivates 76 percent of the best workers. Knowing they have the appreciation of others also is a result of endorsement, motivating 66 percent, and providing opportunities to demonstrate their capability motivates 57 percent.

It's a fact of life that people go where

they are celebrated, not tolerated. Years ago, Bertrand Russell wrote, "A sense of duty is useful in work but offensive in personal relationships. People wish to be liked, not endured with patient resignation." Today, management experts acknowledge that people do better at work when they feel liked, as well. Zig Ziglar says it's part of human nature. Discussing how to touch the hearts of teenagers, Zig says, "Children go where there is excitement, but they stay where there is love." And so it is with us big kids.

As Chris says in *Getting to Know You,* everyone wears an invisible sign that says *Make Me Feel Important!* Managing correctly includes making people feel important by providing endorsement—and appropriate feedback to help them gain it where it is lacking.

So, don't fear discovering your own Endorsement Quotient and the factors that determine it. If your own Endorsement Quotient with another individual is low, expect them to impose additional performance safeguards. If your own Endorsement Quotient is high, you can find out what you're doing and keep doing it! At the same time, you'll become more aware of ways you can grant endorsement to others and help them to achieve it more consistently.

To summarize this chapter:

- Perceptions differ from reality, so we need to distinguish one from the other.

- Our influence may be underrated and its consequences unintended over time.

- "Influentials" create endorsement by investing time and energy in what is important to them, believing they can make a difference.

- When we operate in our circle of influence, it may enlarge to encircle our concerns.

- Our Endorsement Quotient is measurable and can be improved. This requires humility and openness to input that isn't always pleasant to discover.

- We create endorsement with people when we respond with genuine interest, encouragement, and even correction—when they sense that what they do matters.

AFTERWORD: NEXT STEPS

Now that you have finished this study on endorsement, what should you do next? At the risk of sounding obvious, put what you know into practice!

I'm told that seminaries teach Bible students to always ask *So what?* In other words, theological learning means very little unless ministers can help their congregations connect what they know to how they live. It's the same thing here—if endorsement becomes only an item for interesting conversation around the water cooler, you're missing its power in your professional life. If it remains an unpracticed theory in your personal life, you're missing one of the special benefits of relationships.

Chances are, you'll begin experimenting with endorsement concepts in your personal life before you try them out in your workplace anyhow. In the years

that I've been teaching people skills to clients, I've found that's the usual pattern. Certainly, it has been that way when I've introduced DISC and Values. People want to test this information in a safe environment, and they seem to feel they have less to lose in their experimental lab of friendship. However, if you decide to proceed, get moving—show yourself that you can do this!

Doing something beats talking about it almost every time. And it makes sense to keep quiet about what you've learned while you're learning to put it to work in your life. Otherwise, people may mistake your motivations—they may think you've discovered some new idea for manipulating them and greet your actions with suspicion. (As you already know, distrust is not a method for building endorsement!) Instead, just begin doing what you know to do without fanfare. Look for ways you can build people up, demonstrate trust and confidence in them, and deliver what you promise in ways that exceed their expectations.

Practice consistency. Remember that endorsement takes a long time to develop, and it can be destroyed in a short time if you become careless or sloppy in the way you demonstrate trustworthiness. Keep in mind that others' perceptions impact your endorsement—it doesn't matter if your intentions are perfect if your actions and motivations are suspicious.

At the same time, because you understand this information, at least as a theory, you can help others without carrying around undeserved and overwhelming suspicion of others. You're in a position to understand what people need and want, and how to help them get it without manipulation or deception. As Zig says, "You can get anything in the world you want if you help enough other people get what they want." Remember that it's not about trading influence; genuine endorsement must be granted, not negotiated. Yet it's reciprocal in nature, so the way in which you grant it has a lot to do with the way in which you get it.

What else should you do? Read this book again... and then again. We've talked about acquiring endorsement habits, and you'll need reinforcement that will be found as you return to these pages.

As important as understanding how endorsement works, you also need to understand your DISC behavioral style. You can accomplish this in two steps: complete an online, computer-scored Style Assessment and read my book, *Energizing People: Unleashing the Power of DISC*. Both of these are available from Competitive Edge, Inc. (or from our Associates, if that is how you acquired this book).

We also offer the *Personal Interests, Attitudes and Values Assessment* (PIAV), also described in this book, which will help you to understand the six factors that drive your behavior—as DISC explains the "how," PIAV will explain the "why."

ABOUT THE AUTHOR

Judy Suiter is founder and president of Competitive Edge, Inc., located in Peachtree City, Georgia, since 1981. Competitive Edge is recognized internationally as a human resources and training company specializing in candidate selection, executive development and coaching, sales training, and team building. Her firm's motto is, *"Be daring...be first...and be different!"*

Judy is the author of the books **Energizing People: the Power of DISC**, based on the behavioral theories of Dr. William Moulton Marston, and **Exploring Values: Releasing the Power of Attitudes**. She is coauthor of **The Universal Language: DISC Reference Manual**, currently in its ninth printing, and contributed two chapters to **Pleasure and the Quality of Life**.

Judy is a graduate of Middle Tennessee State University with a degree in Industrial and Personnel Psychology and has over 440 hours of advanced behavioral sciences and organizational development. She is a Certified Professional Behavior and Values Analyst (CPBA/CPVA), in addition to designation as a Certified Professional Consultant to Management (CPCM).

Her writing partner for this book is Chris Carey, president of CreativeCommunication, Inc., in Atlanta, Georgia. Chris is a professional member of the National Speakers Association, a Certified Human Behavior Consultant, and author of several books, including **Getting to Know You** and **The Price & the Prize**. He can be reached through www.ChrisCarey.com.

Should you want to purchase additional copies of **THE RIPPLE EFFECT** book for friends or colleagues, they are available at $9.95 each, plus shipping and handling. Discounts are available for quantity purchases.

Energizing People—Unleashing the Power of DISC is the first volume of Judy Suiter's trilogy on human behavior. This book explains the four behavioral types of people you work with and live with—along with each type's preferred ways of dealing with problems, people, pace, and procedures.

- Because DISC is a *predictable* behavior model, this book explains how you behave and what to expect from others, once you understand their behavioral type
- The value of being able to predict your actions and the reactions of other people under different sets of circumstances allows you to have a greater sense of control over your own life
- This understanding is tremendously beneficial in career counseling, conflict management, job matching, succession planning, team building, and stress reduction

---

If you don't know what your values and priorities are, someone else will determine them for you! Just as **Energizing People** explains the "how" of human behavior, **Exploring Values—Releasing the Power of Attitudes**, reveals the "why" that motivates us to do what we do. The second book of Judy's trilogy reveals

- How motivating attitudes and values are developed throughout life
- The six value clusters that have become the core for workplace incentive programs worldwide
- Well-known individuals who demonstrate these values in action
- How to motivate others by understanding their attitudes and values
- Ways to appreciate and work more productively with people who have differing values clusters

Energizing People—Unleashing the Power of DISC and **Exploring Values—Releasing the Power of Attitudes** are available from Competitive Edge for $9.95 each, plus shipping and handling, or from the Associate from whom you purchased this book. Quantity discounts are available.

Managing for Success® is the computer-scored, online behavioral style assessment that unlocks the mystery of your natural and adapted styles by measuring the four factors of DISC. The report, over 20 pages in length, can be delivered to you via e-mail in PDF format, is compatible with any computer, and includes

- General and specific characteristics of your style
- Your value to the organization
- Dos and Don'ts for communicating
- Your ideal environment
- Self-perception and how others perceive you
- Keys to motivating and managing you
- Areas for personal and professional improvement

The applications for this information are unlimited and can be used for sales, customer service, team building, conflict resolution, interpersonal skills, management development, stress management, and marriage and family communication improvement.

Managing for Success® and *Personal Interests, Attitudes and Values* assessments are available online from Competitive Edge at a nominal cost, and group discounts are available.

Competitive Edge, Inc.
P.O. Box 2418 • Peachtree City, GA 30269
Office: (770) 487-6460 • Fax: (770) 487-2919
www.competitiveedgeinc.com
E-mail: judy@competitiveedgeinc.com

We accept Visa, MasterCard, and American Express